The Story of Martha's Vineyard

By
Kevin Shortsleeve

Illustrated by
Elka Iwanowski

A **CAPE COD LIFE** Book
SPECIAL PUBLICATION

Special thanks to
Laura, Robert and Brian.
Joy Hambly
Pat Perry

Library of Congress Catalog Card Number
97-67384
ISBN 0-9622782-6-2
© 1997 by Cape Cod Life Magazine. All Rights reserved. No part of this publication may be reproduced in any form without written consent from the publisher. For information, contact Cape Cod Life, 4 Barlows Landing Road, Unit 14,
P.O. Box 1385 Pocasset, MA 02559

PRINTED IN CANADA

Dedicated to
The "Chappy" Shortsleeves,
Cathy, Mike, Brian, Christine, Cara & Michelle

From the woods to the meadows to the dunes and breeze.
From the harbors and hills to the beetlebung trees.
This fair rolling isle from leeward to windward,
Is known by all sailors as old Martha's Vineyard.

If you like, I will tell you the tales of this land.
Of legends and lores long lost in the sand.

But first we'll go back, so that things will be clear,
To a time when our island was simply... not here...

There was no Martha's Vineyard when this Earth was new,
Just gray empty places, with not much to do.
No oceans, no people, no sea captains' homes,
No church bells or seashells, no Mad Martha's cones.

A bad place to visit. A worse place for walks.
Just rocks, and more rocks, and more rocks... on some rocks.

Volcanic Explosions set fire to the sky,
While a creeping hot river of lava flowed by.

After billions of years the rocks were submerged.
Where the Vineyard would be, an ancient sea surged.

The dinosaurs' ocean was broad, deep and blue,
With beast-like basilosaurs swishing on through.
On a never-ending hunt for something to eat,
These jagged-toothed monsters stretched eighty long feet.

But there came a great change, with the winds blowing cold,
And gone were the waters where the sea serpents rolled.
With snowstorms and windstorms and ice storms and hail,
The Ice Age blew in on a fierce frozen gale.

With more ice and less water,
sea levels went down,
And up rose the land
we would one day call town.

Here mastodons trudged through the deep snowy drifts,
By towering glaciers and vast icy cliffs.

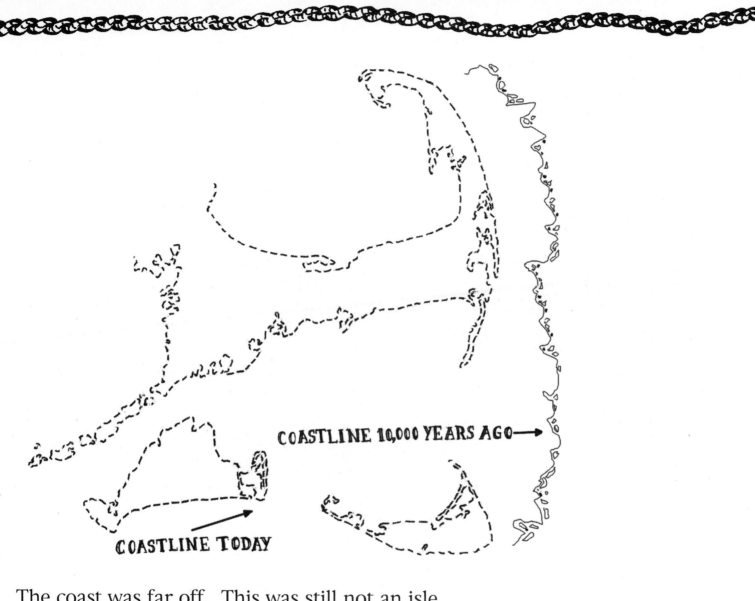

COASTLINE 10,000 YEARS AGO →

COASTLINE TODAY

The coast was far off. This was still not an isle,
A walk to the beach would stretch 70 miles!
To tell you the truth, and I know it sounds odd,
But back then you could walk from here to Cape Cod!

Then out popped the sun and the Ice Age was through,
White fields became green and gray skies became blue.
Forests of flowers welcomed warm weather days.
The ice cliffs collapsed in the sizzling sun's rays.

The glaciers gushed sands in their great melting wake,
Forming lands we would know as the islands and Cape.

Then hunters arrived, walking in from the West.
These were the first people, the first Vineyard guests.
They came seeking deer by trailing their tracks,
Defending their families from bears and wolf packs.

Their lives are a mystery. We know not their names,
But they gathered in fur skins and feasted by flames.
And from their old trash heaps of ashes and powder,
We've learned that they served up a tasty clam chowder!

Still the ice melted, and as you might suppose,
The level of the ocean again slowly rose.
Lowlands were sunk by the new rising tides,
Till finally the Vineyard was cut off on all sides.

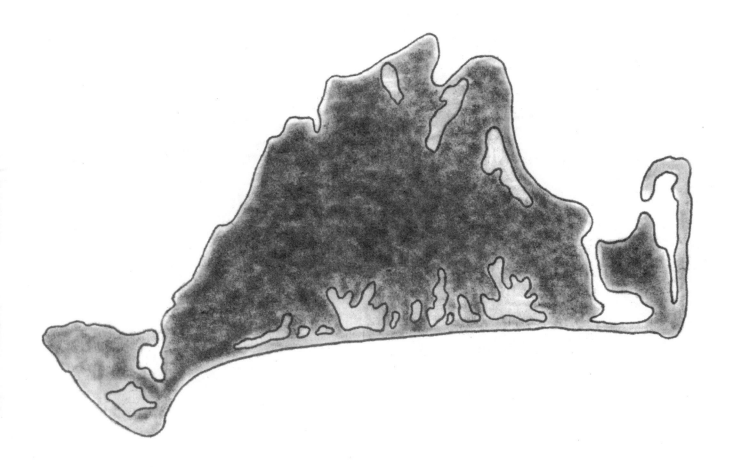

Our Island was born and was here now to stay,
From the bluffs at Gay Head, to Katama's blue bay.

Now finally an island, it had to be named,
"Noepe" -Amid the Water- the people proclaimed.
They titled each corner as they cruised by canoe,
Like Menemsha, Chappaquiddick, Pogue and Tashmoo.

From the dunes of Nobnocket to the shores of Squibnocket
Villages rose from the tribe, Pocanocket.
Creative inventions were tested and born;
Pottery, bow and arrow, small farms to grow corn.

At bedtime their children heard tales of a giant,
Named Maushop the warrior, bold, brave and defiant.
This legend of Gay Head, as told by the tale,
Was so huge, in fact, he could eat a whole whale!
He cooked with tree trunks which were ripped up with ease,
And that's why, they say, Gay Head has no trees!

Many moons rose over old Noepe's shores,
Till some say a strange ship under stripped sail and oars,
brought bold Europeans, who'd braved the deep sea,
To somewhere nearby in 1000 AD.

How strange for the natives,
as they looked on confused,
At these blond bearded men and
their giant canoes.

These were the Vikings, brave sea kings of old,
Leif Ericson leading, so the sagas have told.
For the grapevines which hung from the tall forest wood,
Leif named his discovery "Vinland the Good".

They did not stay long, three years at the most,
Before leaving forever their Vinland outpost.

It could be, however, that right here on M.V.,
Was born the first "paleface" on this side of the sea.
For a Viking named Gudrid, or so goes the story,
Gave birth in Vinland to a boy she named Snorri.
And what if he'd stayed, and not left with the crew?
Does the name "Snorri's Vineyard" sound all right to you?

600 years passed. It was 1602,
When our next guest arrived from the deep ocean blue.
An English sea captain, Bartholomew Gosnold,
in a ship called "The Concord" came searching for gold.

Three thousand miles the good captain had sailed,
Before the jewels of our isle, to him were unveiled.
He did not find gold, but great towering trees,
where grapevines swung slowly in the soft southwest breeze.

"What name," said his crew, "to this vineyard by water?"
He said: "This is Martha's" (perhaps named for his daughter).

They dug sassafras roots, for Gosnold understood,
In England, high prices would be paid for such wood.
They camped on Cuttyhunk. For one month they stayed,
But the crew longed for England, and Gosnold obeyed.

The Concord raised anchor and sailed back 'cross the ocean,
Where the news of their find caused quite a commotion...

Gosnold spoke of riches and of fortunes afar,
So seamen set courses by sextant and star.

In 1607, with a clink and a clanker,
Out rattled the chain of Martin Pring's anchor.
The bay called Katama looked a good place for fish,
So out went his nets with a heave and a swish.
And on Chappaquiddick, where safety seemed surest,
He built a small shelter. Our first summer tourist.

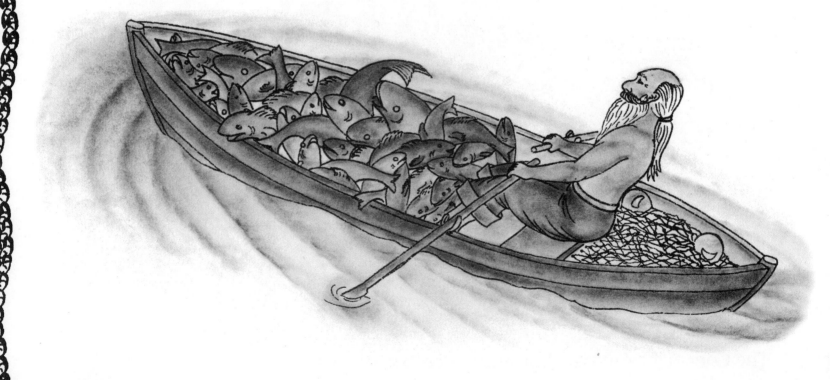

Back in old England, many more raised their sails,
And braved the Atlantic and its fierce frozen gales.
Pilgrims and Puritans, in a search to be free,
Formed a "New" England on this side of the sea.

From Boston and Plymouth these families set sail,
In summers to hunt for the cod and the whale.
They camped on the Vineyard, like old Martin Pring,
And in autumn, to Boston, their catch they would bring.

And then Thomas Mayhew, in 1641,
Landed at Edgartown. The settlers had come.
Unlike Martin Pring, the part-time pioneer,
Mayhew meant to live here four seasons a year.

He went first to the place where the native drum booms,
And there he made friends with the brave Hiacoomes.
Mayhew saw a future where both sides would blend,
The "Redskins" and "Whiteskins" would soon become friends.

At "The Place by the Wayside", now marked with a rock,
The Pocanockets gathered to hear Mayhew talk.
He spoke in their language so that all understood,
His views on religion and man's brotherhood.

The next day, for England,
he sailed off on a trip.
But that was the last time
that they saw Mayhew's ship.

Later, in New England, many farmers would face,
Hard wars with the natives as they fought for more space.
But here, on the Vineyard, where the good Mayhew taught.
Friendship was first in each islander's thought.

Peace on our island was the great legacy,
Of Mayhew, the preacher, who was lost to the sea.

Soon many more settlers stepped on to our shores,
And houses were put up by twos and by fours.
They cleared the tall timber in a hard chopping chore,
Till the ancient high forest was lost evermore.
Now pastures appeared for the wool-bearing sheep.
And our rolling green hills were here now to keep.

The buzzing of saws and the hammer blow's clang,
Gave rise to new villages where church bells soon rang.
For farmer and fisherman, street sweeper and wife,
Hard work filled the days of colonial life.
Many learned how to fish in Madakessett Creek,
By watching the ways of the natives' technique.
They farmed corn, wheat and barley to make oats and malt,
And from dried up sea water, they harvested salt.
The largest candle works in America they say,
Was old Fisher's Candles by Edgartown's bay.

Once upon a time, out at Robinson's Hole,
A story was told on a night black as coal,
Of a farmer who answered a knock at the door,
And a ragged old man who fell in on the floor.

This mumbling sailor was placed in a bed,
The good farmer listened as the tired man said…

"I'll tell ye a tale what'll make ya quite glad.
I served with a pirate when I was a wee lad.
That old Captain Kidd was me commander and chief,
'Tis the truth of it stranger. I sailed with that thief!
Eiy, many years ago" the coughing man said,
"On Nomansland Island, just south o' Gay Head,
Me commander and me dug deep with a spade,
And hid for safe keeping, gold, rubies and jade.
But Kidd went to prison, that blimey old sap,
So now I've returned to get rich with me map.
But alas", he went on, "tis the last of me treks!"
Then he died before scratching his map with an "X".

Since then many seekers have snooped through the hills,
Of Nomansland Island, but with no luck or thrills.
And today it could be that still somewhere is hid,
The lost golden treasure of a pirate named Kidd.

In April of 1775,
The War of Independence finally arrived.
To be our own country was the bold rebel call,
To be rid of "Old" England once and for all.
Our men grabbed their muskets and sailed off in their boats,
To join George Washington and fight the Red Coats.

Martha's Vineyard was left with no one to guard,
If the British should come and decide to bombard…

Well, the enemy did land, with frigates and sloops.
Eighty-two ships and some ten thousand troops!
They crowded onto shore to steal what they could.
They took coal and lamp oil and freshly chopped wood.
Smashing windows and doors in a dark rotten mood,
They emptied our cupboards to the last drop of food.
Handfuls of silver dropped in their deep pockets,
As well as fine jewelry, gold bracelets and lockets.
They ripped up our corn and our wheat by the tons.
They sank thirty-two ships and stole four hundred guns.

And the last thing added to the huge stolen heap,
Was three hundred cows and ten thousand sheep!

On the mainland, however, our boys wouldn't budge.
And England surrendered, sailing home with a grudge.
With the war at an end, we were proud to proclaim,
The United States of America was our new name.

The enemy now gone, we could feel free to sail,
And hunt the Seven Seas in search of the whale...

Edgartown harbor and its old docks and slips,
At one time was home port to fifty whale ships.
From the frozen far reaches of the north polar bear,
To the tropical steam of the crocodile's lair,
Brave Vineyard whalers, with their broad sails unfurled,
Cruised every ocean which is known to this world.

Pocanocket natives who sailed with the schooners,
Were known the world over as expert harpooners.

There once was a preacher who stood on Oak Bluffs,
He watched the seas rolling and the sky's cloudy puffs.
And he thought, as he sipped from a stream a cool drink,
"No place could be better to preach and to think."
And so every summer,
in the sweet solitude,
he'd come with his parish
to enjoy the soft mood.

Many thousands soon joined in these prayerful events,
With picnics and singalongs and lanterns and tents.

Gingerbread cottages sprung up all around,
With rocking chair porches looking out on the Sound.

But the best thing by far which sprang from the sites,
Was the last day of meetings, when up went the lights.
Like Christmas in summer, bulbs hung from the eaves,
And twinkled bright colors as they bobbed in the breeze.

To get to camp meetings where the faithful would kneel,
There came the great steamers with their huge paddle wheels.
So for the first time, you could depend on a ride,
Which sailed on a schedule, no matter the tide.

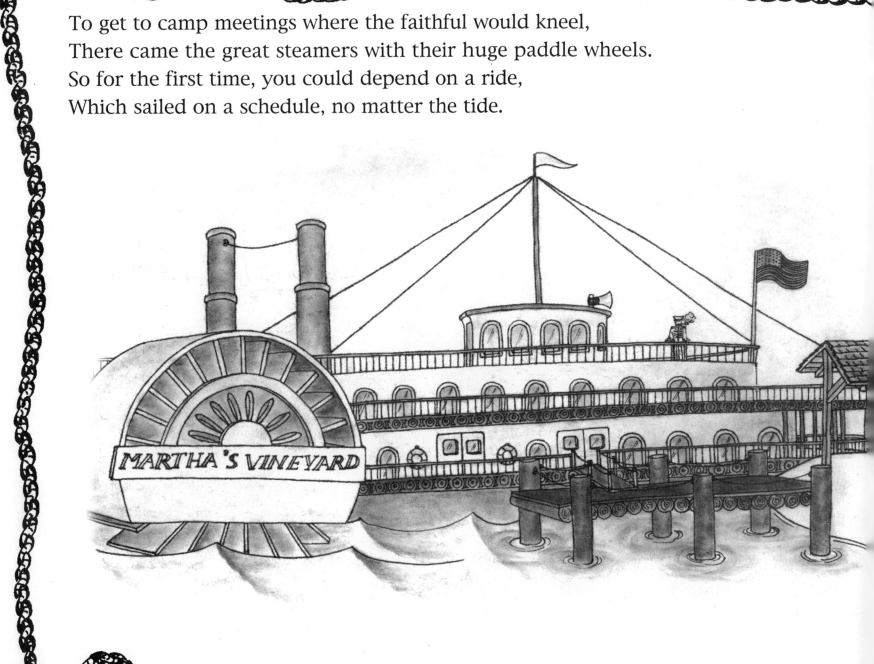

Before there were autos and long before planes.
You could travel the island by rail riding trains.

You boarded your choo-choo not far from the ferry,
And chugged from Oak Bluffs to South Beach or Tisbury.

Do you know the old way we used to get news,
Before e-mail, of course, and before TV too?

On old Chappaquiddick, perched up on a bluff,
We flew colored flags in the soft windy puffs.

On a hill on Nantucket flags flew just the same,
With signals we'd read as our spyglass took aim.

Each flag had a meaning which we all knew by sight,
Like "Storm Comin' in." or "Are you free Friday night?"

There were many ships lost on the old Vineyard coast,
On the swift shifting sand bars of riptides and ghosts.

The natives say Maushop once built a stone ridge,
With boulders we know as the dark "Devils Bridge".
Huge jagged green rocks jutting out from Gay Head,
Left there by the giant, so the legend has said.
To ships the world over, this ridge was a scourge,
As vessels ripped open and in the sea surged.

The "City of Columbus" in 1894,
Lost all those aboard as she sank to the floor.

The natives of Gay Head looked out from the cliffs,
To Devil's Bridge waters where the whirling wind whips.
When a stormy sea loomed, the squad would make checks,
And rush to the rescue at the first sight of wrecks.
They'd launch open boats into great crashing waves,
And snatch lucky sailors from their Devil's Bridge graves.

When "The Galena" went down, the frantic crew waved,
So the rescue squad launched and all hands were saved.

One evening one summer, when the skies were quite dark,
A factory on Main Street set off a small spark,
Which burst forth into flames and leaped door to door,
As building after building was lost in the roar.
Old Main Street and Beech Street burned straight to the ground.
The next day not a church nor a house could be found.
Forty acres of trees with their shady pleasures,
Seventy-two homes and their family treasures.
Vineyard Haven was ruined, not much left to see.
So burned the great fire of 1883.

There came to this island where legends are made,
Joshua Slocum, a sea captain by trade,
Whose plan was, it seems, since the day of his birth,
To sail by himself, alone 'round the Earth!

They called Slocum "Crazy! Not in one million days!"
You'll be shipwrecked and sunk! You'll be washed to the waves!"

But Slocum thought maybe he knew what was best, And he crossed the Atlantic, then headed southwest.

He guided his sloop more than 900 days,
A thirty-seven footer, well known as the "The Spray".
To Brazil, the Horn and Pacific south seas,
To Sydney, Africa, and Florida's Keys.

Slocum had done it. The first man all alone.
He sailed clear 'round the globe and finally was home.
And of all the wide world, every port and empire,
The Vineyard was where Slocum chose to retire.

Then came the inventions, like the flick of a switch,
Machines which could push things and wash things and stitch.
Tube radio signals beamed in through the air,
And electrified lighting clicked on like a flare.
Gas motors turned axles, axles turned tires,
Tires turned swiftly under new fangled flyers.
Toasters popped toast up and Bell telephones rang,
And hand cranked phonographs soon suddenly sang!

So, like the wide world and its new modern age,
The history of our island turned a new page.
From the side of the road, the forgotten horse peered,
And harbor scenes changed as tall ships disappeared.

When World War One started, the enemy had tricks,
Like a huge German sub called a "156",
Which rose in the waters of Nantucket Sound,
Aimed her guns at a tugboat and started to pound.

Although the "Perth Amboy" was battered to the brink,
And burned to a crisp, the old tug didn't sink!
The captain and crew, amid wondering stares,
chugged in to the Vineyard for rest and repairs.

When World War Two started more shells would explode,
As bombers flew over and dumped out their load.
We watched from Gay Head from atop the tall highland,
As the Navy held practice on Nomansland Island.
The planes would swoop down in a rip-roaring blitz,
And a piece of Nomans' would explode into bits.

Bombs were not the only big things to blast down,
As hurricanes swirled up and came bursting through town.

In 1938 the worst storm ever known,
Blew ships from the harbors and dropped them on homes.
With gusts blowing harder with each thunder stroke,
Wind meters spun madly. At 150, they broke!

Out on Chappaquiddick the roads turned to mud.
As the outer beach sank in the huge foaming flood.
Another wave fell and the beach washed away!
An island now truly! Cut off by a bay!

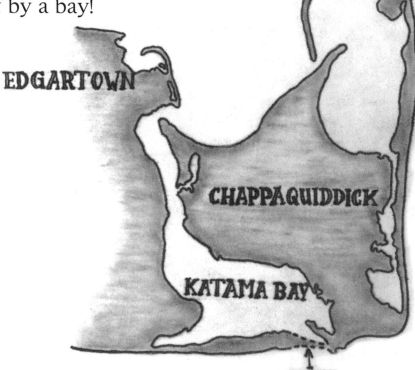

As time travels onward, big storms come and go,
And the barrier beach shifts with each mighty blow.
That's why old "Chappy" is an odd sort of spot,
One year it's an island, the next year it's not!

Though sometimes a storm would blow off their roof racks,
Many tourists still came here to rest and relax.
More buses, more mopeds, more cars pulling boats,
More of all things in harbors that sink, swim or floats.

For the last forty years, the sea gulls and deer,
Have had more human neighbors move in every year.

With people came houses and driveways and shops,
Fancy vacation homes with antennas on tops.
Each house needed space. Each space took up land,
Each lot advertised as the best strip of sand.

So the towns put their foot down and took back control,
And "good conservation" was the island's new goal.
To pick out some land for all people to share,
And to outline some rules about who will build where.

Henry Beetle Hough perhaps cared more than most,
He loved the old island and its soothing seacoast.
The Vineyard Gazette was the paper he ran,
And when things needed saying, Hough was the man.
He wrote many great books all about Vineyard life,
And gave us, as a gift, from him and his wife,
Huge plots of their land that no tractor may trample.
Hough lived by his conscience and set the example.

The Vineyard's year-round and part-time summer residents,
Include famous first ladies, rock stars and presidents.
Many artists and writers and others well known,
Are inclined to agree that this makes a good home.
Big stars and directors shoot films here because,
It's simply so charming. (Perhaps you've seen "Jaws"?)

You'll see them out jogging by their sea-side chalets
Or lunching with agents at outdoor cafes.

Although rather quiet, reserved and low-key,
This place is more famous than one person can be.
In fact all the world over, the Vineyard has fame,
Unmatched by most islands with sizes the same.

Our foreign ambassador, the famous Black Dog,
Is known from Beijing to the green Scottish bog.

Today on the Vineyard great fun can be found.
You can bike to the beaches or sail on the Sound,
Hold tight to your steed on the old Flying Horses,
Or ride the real thing through a forest of courses.
Takemmy Farm is the home of some llamas,
Miniature donkeys and their miniature mammas.
The state hatchery has some lobsters to meet.
You can para-sail, windsurf or ski on bare feet.
Fairgrounds and fireworks make warm summer pleasure.
And sea glass is found by searchers of treasure,
But if that's not quite how you'd plan fun escapes,
Then do like the Vikings…

Now watch the waves crashing and shifting the sand.
Feel the Zephyr's wind pass and reshape the land.
Remember our island as it is and it was,
From the basilosaur's roar to the motorboats' buzz.
Remember as you walk and hear a bell striking,
On this place stood a native, a pirate, a Viking.

As you see the fog lift to reveal quiet deer,
As the morning mist rolls before blue skies appear,
Think back on the story of the woods and the shores,
And know that the future of the Vineyard is yours.

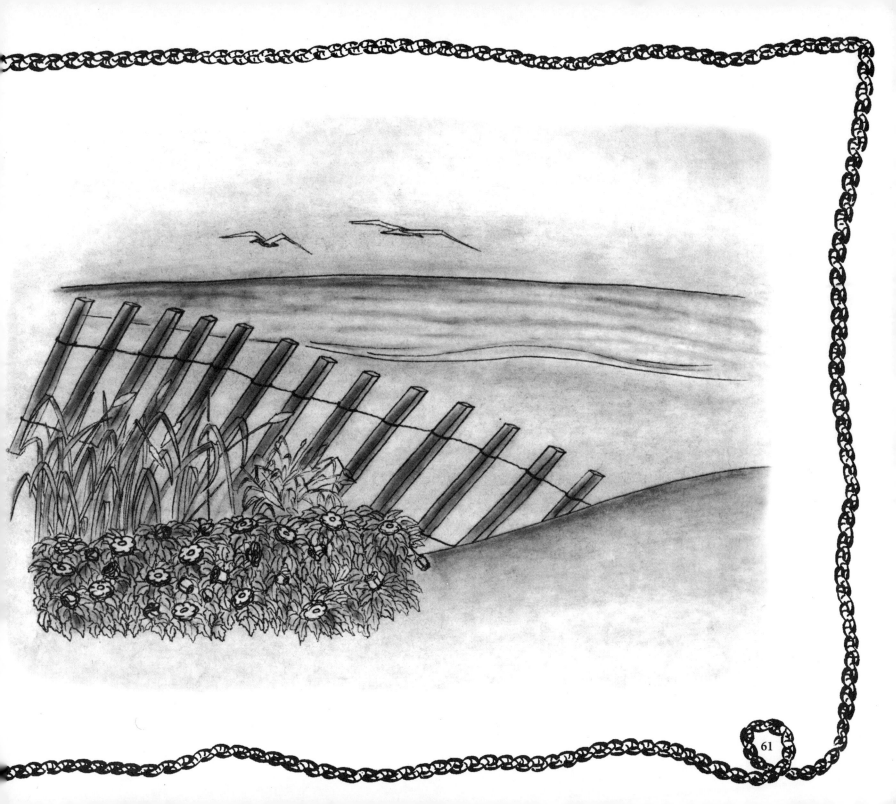

The Story of Martha's Vineyard

Prehistory
60 million BC.   An ocean covers the entire region.
16,000-10,000 B.C.   The Ice Age. Ocean recedes. Coastline 70 miles to the east.
10,000-9,000 B.C.   First evidence of humans inhabiting the region. Paleolithic man.
9,000-3,000 B.C.   Archaic period. Hunter/gatherers.
5,000-3,000 B.C.   Oceans rise again, cutting off the mainland and forming the island.
3,000 B.C.-1500 A.D.   Woodland Period. Development of pottery, crops & weapons.
550-1600   Irish, Bretton and Basque fisherman explore the North Atlantic with a possible landfall at Martha's Vineyard.
1001   Leif Ericson discovers "Vinland"
1002   Thorwald Ericson visits Vinland.
1010-1013   Thorfin Karlsefni establishes a temporary settlement in Vinland.

Age of Exploration.
(with events and listings of those who sighted and/or explored the island prior to the arrival of Thomas Mayhew.)
1498   John Cabot, for England.
1509   Sebastian Cabot, for England.
1524   Giovanni da Verrazano, for France, names the island "Claudia."
1525   Estevan Gomez for Spain.
1600   A large group of Wampanoags gather for a pow wow on Martha's Vineyard.
1602   Bartholomew Gosnold, for England, maps and names "Martha's Vineyard." Makes a failed attempt to create the first settlement in North America on Cuttyhunk Island.
1605   George Waymouth, for England.
1605-1606   Samuel de Champlain for France.
1606   Martha's Vineyard granted to Sir Fernando Georges & Alexander, Earl of Sterling.
1607   Captain Martin Pring begins regular trade with the natives on Martha's Vineyard. Names Katama Bay "Whitsun Bay", and the bluff on Chappaquiddick, "Mount Aldworth". Built a small stockade on Chappaquiddick.
1609   Henry Hudson for the Dutch.
1610   "The Tempest" by William Shakespeare is first performed. Some believe Shakespeare was heavily influenced by descriptions of Martha's Vineyard and Cuttyhunk detailed to him by his friend Bartholomew Gosnold.
1611   Edward Harlow for England.
1614-1615   Captain Thomas Hunt, captures 24 natives from the Cape and islands. Most are sold as slaves in Spain. The island native Epenow manages to escape from England and return to Martha's Vineyard.
1620   Plymouth Colony founded.
1627   Aptucxet Trading Post opens on Cape Cod.
1630s   Families from Boston and Watertown, the Trapps, the Vincents, the Peaces and the Stones, begin to camp here when fishing.

Settlement and Colonial Life
1641   Martha's Vineyard purchased for 40 pounds by Thomas Mayhew Sr. His son, Thomas Mayhew Jr., arrives on the island with the intention of establishing a settlement.
1642   80 settlers arrive from the Merrimack Valley. A village is built on the shores of "Great Harbor".
1651   Peter Folger (Benjamin Franklin's grandfather) establishes a school for the island natives.
1657   Thomas Mayhew Jr., after delivering his speech at "The Place by the Wayside", is lost at sea.
1659   The Indian settlement of Christiantown established.
1660   The Daggett House opens up for business.
1668   Chappaquiddick, Nomansland and Martha's Vineyard become Dukes County.
1671   Martha's Vineyard officially becomes part of the colony of New York.
1671   The towns of Edgartown, Tisbury and Chilmark are established.
1671   The town of Great Harbor changes its name to "Edgar Towne".
1672   The Vincent House, of Edgartown, is constructed. Now the oldest building on the island.
1675   King Philip's War. This war pitted the colonists of southern New England against the natives. Martha's Vineyard Indians did not join in the fighting.
1681   Reservation established at Gay Head for the native islanders.
1691   The Island is acquired by The Massachusetts Bay Colony.
1699   Captain Kidd hides a treasure, perhaps, on Nomansland Island.
c.1710   The pirate Blackbeard reportedly hides a treasure at Blue Rock on Chappaquiddick, only to come back and retrieve it several years later.
1727   An earthquake rocks the island for one full minute.
1737   A rare display of The Northern Lights is witnessed by many islanders.
1765   The first whale ship on the island, "The Lidia", sets sail for Davis Straits.
1769   Tashmoo Farm built.
1774   British close Boston Harbor. Edgartown boycotts Great Britain.

The American Revolution to 1899.
1775-1781   The American Revolution.
1775   Local teenagers destroy The Liberty Pole in an act of defiance against the British.
1776   Martha's Vineyard declares itself neutral in the conflict; however, many islanders head to the mainland to fight the British.
1777   John Paul Jones captures two British ships in Vineyard Haven.
1777   Defiant Islanders produce The Declaration of Rights.
1778   British troops steal nearly all the provisions and livestock on the island.
1799   Gay Head Light constructed.
1800s   Thaxter Academy, of Edgartown is the main school of higher learning for Martha's Vineyard and Nantucket residents.
1802   Cape Pogue Light constructed.
1812   War of 1812. Iron mined on the Vineyard is used to build "Old Ironsides".
1814   The Pagoda Tree in Edgartown is planted.
1816   For the first time, a Vineyard whaleship sails for the Pacific Ocean.
1817   West Chop Light House constructed.
1818   Steamships begin regular service between Martha's Vineyard and Cape Cod.
1820-1860   The Great Whaling Age of Martha's Vineyard.
1827   First Methodist Camp Meeting on the island.
1830-1870   Daniel Fisher Candle Company in operation.
1835   First camp meeting at Oak Bluffs. Nine tents and a preacher stand.
1837   Nathaniel Hawthorne publishes his "Twice Told Tales", written while vacationing in Edgartown.
1845-1870   The Chilmark brick mill in operation.
1850   The paint mill which utilized Gay Head's colorful clay begins operation.
1850   Heyday of whaling. Edgartown Harbor is home port to 50 whale ships.
1855   The Vineyard Gazette first published.
1859   The first annual Agricultural Society Fair and Livestock Show.
1859   Petroleum begins to become more popular than whale oil.
1859   The first "gingerbread" cottage is built in Oak Bluffs.

1860	Harper's magazine publishes an article on the island reporting that up to 12,000 visitors attend the daily meetings at Oak Bluffs.
1860-1865	The American Civil War. 240 soldiers serve from Martha's Vineyard.
1864	The Elizabeth Islands separate from the town of Chilmark.
1869	First organized illumination night.
1870	The town of Gay Head officially established.
1871	Holme's Hole changes its name to Vineyard Haven.
1874	President Grant attends a camp meeting at Oak Bluffs.
1874-1897	A Railroad runs between Tisbury, Oak Bluffs, Edgartown, and South Beach.
1876	The Flying Horses carousel installed. Now the oldest carousel in the United States.
1877	East Chop Light House constructed.
1879	The Tabernacle is constructed in Trinity Park.
1880	The town of Cottage City Established.
1883	The Great Fire of 1883 destroys most of Vineyard Haven.
1884	Largest Sperm Whale ever caught is captured by "The Alaska" of Edgartown. Produced 168 barrels of oil.
1884	Wreck of the steamer "City of Columbus". 121 perish in the waters off Gay Head.
1890	A street car system pulled by horses is implemented on the island.
1891	Wreck of "The Galena". All hands saved by the Gay Head Indians.
1892	West Tisbury and Vineyard Haven officially separate from the town of Tisbury.
1898	Joshua Slocum returns from his voyage and settles on Martha's Vineyard.
1898	The Gale of 1898 destroys 50 ships in Vineyard Haven.

<u>20th Century</u>

1901	Monument erected in remembrance of Thomas Mayhew Jr. at "The Place By the Wayside".
1902	Monument erected on Cuttyhunk to commemorate the 300th anniversary of Bartholomew Gosnold's landing.
1907	Joshua Slocum lost at sea.
1907	Cottage City changes its name to Oak Bluffs.
1914	The Cape Cod Canal is opened. Shipping industries on island are devastated.
1914-1918	World War I. Gay Head supplies the highest percentage of volunteers of any town in the United States.
1916	The Vineyard Plain, from Edgartown to Tisbury, burns in a massive forest fire.
1917	The tug "Perth Amboy" is nearly destroyed by a German submarine.
1917	The song "Tivoli Girl", inspired by the festivities at Oak Bluffs, is among the most popular songs in the United States.
1917	The horses are removed and the streetcars are electrified.
1920s-1930s	Artists, writers and other "radicals" begin to frequent the Barn House in Chilmark.
1938	Worst Hurricane in the history of the Island. Includes 150 mile per hour winds and a twelve foot tidal wave.
1941-1945	World War Two. Nomansland Island used for target practice by the Navy.
1944	Hurricane of 1944.
1946	The first Striped Bass and Bluefish Derby.
1954	Hurricane of 1954.
1958	The "Andrea Doria" sinks in the waters off Martha's Vineyard.
1959	Sheriff's Meadow Foundation Chartered.
1966	The Cold War comedy about Martha's Vineyard, "The Russians are Coming, the Russians are Coming", is nominated for several Oscars.
1969	Senator Edward Kennedy has his accident on Chappaquiddick.
1971	The Black Dog Tavern opens.
1971	Chicama Vineyards begins producing wine.
1974	The song "Mockingbird" recorded by island residents Carly Simon and James Taylor, is a top ten hit.
1975	Steven Spielberg directs the film "Jaws", filmed on Martha's Vineyard.
1978	The first Tivoli Day.
1983	The original "Black Dog" dies at age 15.
1984	WMVY radio commences broadcast.
1984	Death of Henry Beetle Hough, the "Conscience of Martha's Vineyard".
1985	Hurricane Bell.
1991	Hurricane Bob.
1992	The QE II is grounded off Gay Head.
1993	President Clinton spends his summer holiday on the island.
1994	Princess Diana spends a vacation on the island.
1995	"Livestock", an exclusive concert for island residents only, features performances by local icons, James Taylor and Carly Simon.

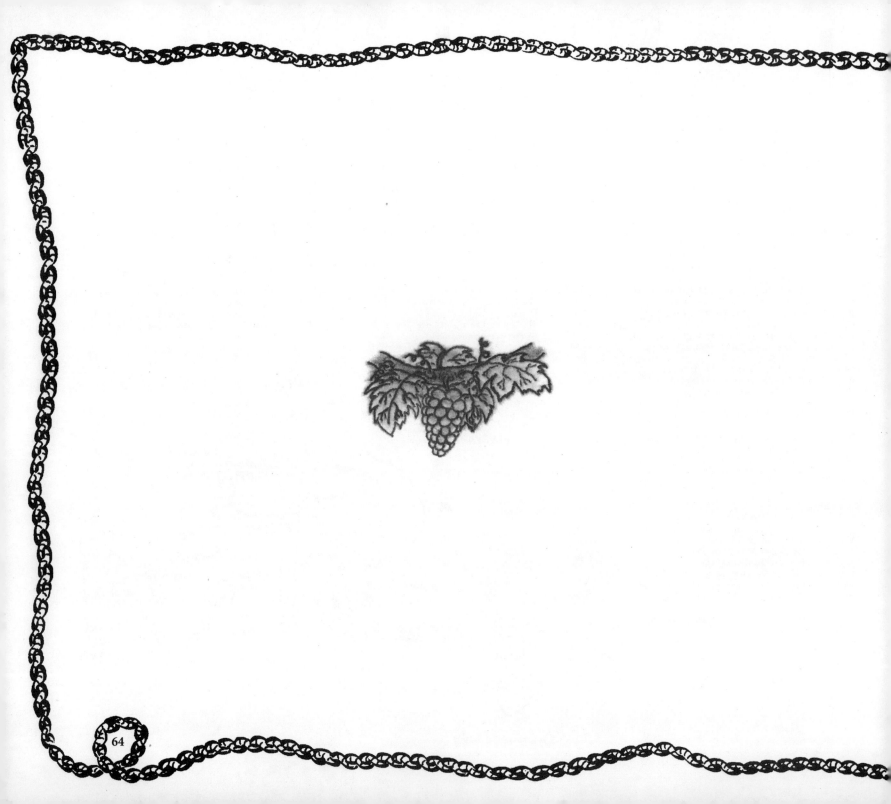